# WOODPELLET

# SMOKER & GRILL

# COOKBOOK

## -The Ultimate Cookbook With the Best Barbecue Recipes -

*[Richard Lyons]*

# Table Of Content

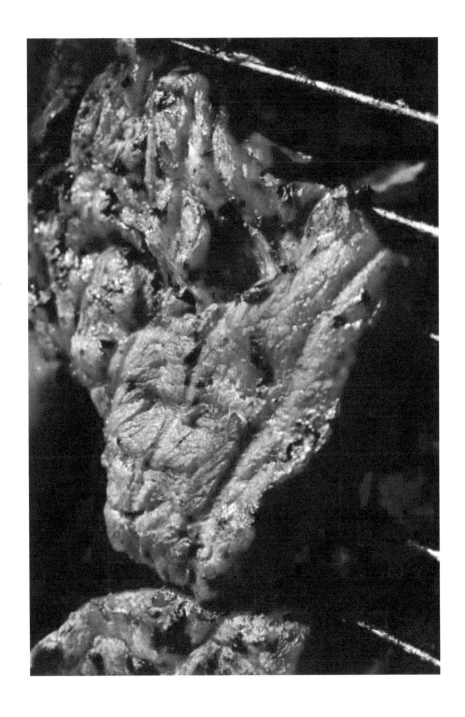

The following Book is reproduced below with the goal of providing information that is as accurate and reliable as possible. Regardless, purchasing this Book can be seen as consent to the fact that both the publisher and the author of this book are in no way experts on the topics discussed within and that any recommendations or suggestions that are made herein are for entertainment purposes only. Professionals should be consulted as needed prior to undertaking any of the action endorsed herein.

This declaration is deemed fair and valid by both the American Bar Association and the Committee of Publishers Association and is legally binding throughout the United States.

Furthermore, the transmission, duplication, or reproduction of any of the following work including specific information will be considered an illegal act irrespective of if it is done electronically or in print. This extends to creating a secondary or tertiary copy of the work or a recorded copy and is only allowed with the express written consent from the Publisher. All additional right reserved.

The information in the following pages is broadly considered a truthful and accurate account of facts and as such, any inattention, use, or misuse of the information in question by the reader will render any resulting actions solely under their purview. There are no scenarios in which the publisher or the original author of this work can be in any fashion deemed liable for any hardship or damages that may befall them after undertaking information described herein.

Additionally, the information in the following pages is intended only for informational purposes and should thus be thought of as universal. As befitting its nature, it is presented without assurance regarding its prolonged validity or interim quality. Trademarks that are mentioned are done without written consent and can in no way be considered an endorsement from the trademark holder.

# CHAPTER 1: **GRILL BEEF**

## -LONDON BROIL

**Prep Time:**
25 mins
**Cook Time:**
30 mins
**Total Time:**
55 mins
**Servings:**
6
**Yield:**
6 servings

3 tablespoons crumbled blue cheese
2 tablespoons butter, softened
1 teaspoon fresh chives (Optional)
1 tablespoon coarsely ground black pepper
1 teaspoon garlic salt
1 teaspoon onion powder
¼ teaspoon ground cayenne pepper
1 (2 pound) beef flank steak
2 tablespoons olive oil, divided

1
Preheat the grill for low heat.

2
In a bowl, mix the blue cheese, butter, and chives. Set aside. In a separate bowl, mix the black pepper, garlic salt, onion powder, and cayenne pepper.

3

Rub the steak with olive oil. Coat both sides of the meat with the spice mixture, and rub in by hand or press with a spatula.

4

Lightly oil the grill grate. Place meat on the grill, and cook 10 to 15 minutes per side, or to desired doneness. Grill to rare or medium rare for best flavor. Remove from grill, and slice lengthwise into thin strips. Top with a large dollop of blue cheese butter, and serve.

**NUTRITION::**
227 calories; protein 19.4g; carbohydrates 1.2g; fat 15.8g; cholesterol 47.1mg; sodium 424mg

## -SMOKED AND PULLED BEEF

**Prep Time:**
30 mins
**Cook Time:**
4 hrs 5 mins
Additional:
30 mins
**Total Time:**
5 hrs 5 mins
**Servings:**
6
**Yield:**
6 servings

5 tablespoons dark brown sugar
4 ½ teaspoons garlic powder
4 ½ teaspoons onion powder
4 teaspoons paprika
4 teaspoons seasoned salt (such as LAWRY'S®)
1 tablespoon ground black pepper
2 teaspoons ground cumin
1 teaspoon ground cayenne pepper
3 ½ pounds bone-in Boston butt roast
½ cup spicy brown mustard
1 cup pickle juice
¾ cup olive oil
charcoal
8 pounds fruit wood chunks for smoking
2 cups pilsner-style beer (such as Budweiser®)
4 ¼ cups water, or as needed

1

Mix brown sugar, garlic powder, onion powder, paprika, seasoned salt, black pepper, cumin, and cayenne pepper together in a small bowl to make dry rub.

2

Coat roast with spicy brown mustard. Sprinkle dry rub all over roast and work it into all the folds and creases.

3

Combine pickle juice and olive oil in a small bowl.

4

Preheat 5 pounds charcoal in a smoker according to manufacturer's instructions until white and flaming. Distribute 7 to 8 large wood chunks over the coals. Place a drip pan on top; pour in beer and enough water to fill the pan most of the way. Close smoker; bring liquid in the drip pan to a boil. Place roast on top and close smoker.

5

Smoke roast, turning every hour, until browned, about 2 hours. Baste roast with pickle juice and olive mixture. Continue smoking, turning and basting every hour, until an instant-read thermometer inserted in the center reads 175 degrees F (80 degrees C), 2 to 3 hours more.

6

Remove roast from smoker and wrap with aluminum foil. Let rest, about 30 minutes.

7

Uncover roast and cut into chunks. Shred chunks into small strands; transfer to a large bowl. Squeeze strands with both hands repeatedly, mixing after each squeeze

**NUTRITION::**

700 calories; protein 29.6g; carbohydrates 20.6g; fat 53.5g; cholesterol 104.1mg; sodium 965.3mg.

## -CORNED BEEF AND CABBAGE

**Prep Time:**
10 mins
**Cook Time:**
2 hrs 25 mins
**Total Time:**
2 hrs 35 mins
**Servings:**
5
**Yield:**
5 servings

3 pounds corned beef brisket with spice packet
10 small red potatoes
5 carrots, peeled and cut into 3-inch pieces
1 large head cabbage, cut into small wedges

1

Place corned beef in large pot or Dutch oven and cover with water. Add the spice packet that came with the corned beef. Cover pot and bring to a boil, then reduce to a simmer. Simmer approximately 50 minutes per pound or until tender.

2

Add whole potatoes and carrots, and cook until the vegetables are almost tender. Add cabbage and cook for 15 more minutes. Remove meat and let rest 15 minutes.

3

Place vegetables in a bowl and cover. Add as much broth (cooking liquid reserved in the Dutch oven or large pot) as you want. Slice meat across the grain.

**NUTRITION::**

839 calories; protein 49.6g; carbohydrates 68.9g; fat 41.3g; cholesterol 147mg; sodium 3377.5mg.

# CHAPTER 2: PORK RECIPE

## -COUNTRY RIBS

**Prep Time:**
10 mins
**Cook Time:**
1 hr 45 mins
**Total Time:**
1 hr 55 mins
**Servings:**
6
**Yield:**
6 servings

¾ cup cold water
¾ cup ketchup
2 tablespoons vinegar
2 tablespoons Worcestershire sauce
1 tablespoon salt, or to taste
1 tablespoon paprika
1 teaspoon chili powder
½ teaspoon cracked black pepper
1 (4 pound) package country-style pork ribs
water, to cover

1

Stir cold water, ketchup, vinegar, Worcestershire sauce, salt, paprika, chili powder, and black pepper together in a large pot. Add ribs to the pot. Pour enough water into the pot to cover the ribs completely.

2

Bring the water to a boil, reduce heat to medium-low, and cook at a simmer until ribs are tender, about 90 minutes.

3

Preheat an outdoor grill for medium-high heat and lightly oil the grate.

4

Cook ribs on preheated grill, basting frequently with sauce, until browned, 12 to 15 minutes.

**NUTRITION::**

366 calories; protein 36g; carbohydrates 9.6g; fat 19.9g; cholesterol 123.1mg; sodium 1615.6mg.

# -CLASSIC PULLED PORK

**Prep Time:**
15 mins
**Cook Time:**
8 hrs
**Total Time:**
8 hrs 15 mins
**Servings:**
10
**Yield:**
10 servings

1 onion, thinly sliced
4 ½ pounds bone-in pork loin end roast
salt and ground black pepper to taste
¾ cup cider vinegar
¼ cup water
½ (18 ounce) bottle hickory brown sugar barbeque sauce
3 tablespoons brown sugar, or to taste

1
Arrange onion slices in the bottom of a slow cooker. Season pork with salt and pepper and place over onion. Add vinegar and water.

2
Cook pork on Low for 8 hours. Transfer pork to a platter and shred with two forks. Remove and discard about half the pork juices from slow cooker and stir in shredded pork, barbeque sauce, and brown sugar.

## NUTRITION::

270 calories; protein 23.6g; carbohydrates 14.3g; fat 12.1g; cholesterol 71.4mg; sodium 340.9mg

## -BARBECUED PIG

**Prep Time:**
1 hr
**Cook Time:**
7 hrs
Additional:
12 hrs
**Total Time:**
20 hrs
**Servings:**
48
**Yield:**
1 suckling pig

2 cups vegetable oil
1 cup achiote (annatto) seeds
24 cloves garlic, peeled
3 tablespoons dried oregano
¾ cup salt
½ cup sour orange juice
1 whole (25 pound) suckling pig, dressed
16 cloves chopped garlic
16 peppercorns
12 fresh jalapeno pepper, seeded
2 cups extra virgin olive oil
1 cup distilled white vinegar
1 cup lime juice
2 tablespoons salt
Cheesecloth

**1**

Annatto Oil: In a small saucepan, heat oil over low heat. Stir in annatto seeds, and cook for about 5 minutes, stirring occasionally. Cool, and strain it before use, removing the seeds.

**2**

In a large mortar, crush 24 cloves garlic with oregano and 3/4 cup salt. Stir in the sour orange juice. Set aside.

**3**

Make deep cuts in the pig on the neck, just under the lower jaw, on the loin, legs, shoulders, and ribs. Rub the seasoned orange juice into the cuts, as well as all over the skin, and in the cavity of the pig. Cover the pig with cheesecloth, and refrigerate overnight.

**4**

Build an open charcoal fire over a bed of stones. Hot coals may need to be added during the long cooking period. Place a post with a Y shape on either end of the fire.

**5**

Pass a smooth pole with no bark through the body of the pig. Tie the front legs tightly around the pole. Do the same with the hind legs, stretching them as far as possible. Resting the ends of the pole on the Y posts, place the pig over hot coals. Rotate the pole constantly and slowly in order to cook the pig evenly, and baste it frequently with the annatto oil. Roast the pig for about seven hours, or until a thermometer stuck into the thickest part of the thigh reaches 145 degrees F (63 degrees C). Carve.

6

Meanwhile, prepare the garlic sauce by first crushing the remaining 16 cloves garlic, the 16 peppercorns, and the fresh chilies in a mortar. Transfer mixture to a small bowl. Stir in olive oil, vinegar, lime juice, and 2 tablespoons salt. Serve with carved meat.

## Nutrition:

Per Serving: 602 calories; protein 16.1g; carbohydrates 3.5g; fat 57.9g; cholesterol 82.9mg; sodium 338.8mg

# -CRISPY PORK BELLY

**Prep Time:**
10 mins
**Cook Time:**
6 hrs 5 mins
Additional:
8 hrs
**Total Time:**
14 hrs 15 mins
**Servings:**
6
**Yield:**
6 servings

½ pound whole pork belly, skin removed
½ teaspoon smoked paprika, or to taste
kosher salt and ground black pepper to taste
1 tablespoon olive oil, or to taste

1
Preheat oven to 200 degrees F (95 degrees C).

2
Season pork belly all over with smoked paprika, salt, and black pepper. Wrap pork in parchment paper; wrap a second time in aluminum foil, and a third time in another sheet of aluminum foil. Place pork packet in a baking dish.

3
Roast in the preheated oven until tender for 6 hours. Let cool in wrappings to room temperature; place cooled packet in refrigerator and chill for 8 hours or overnight.

4

Unwrap chilled meat. Save any rendered fat that falls away when unwrapping pork.

5

Cut meat into 6 equal-size portions. Cut 1/8-inch by 1/8-inch slashes in the fat-side of the pork. Season with salt.

6

Heat 2 tablespoons reserved pork fat in a skillet over medium heat. Place pork belly, fat side down, in hot fat; cook until well-browned on all sides and heated through, 5 to 10 minutes. Transfer pork belly to a plate, drizzle with olive oil and season with pepper.

**Nutrition:**

Per Serving: 87 calories; protein 4.6g; carbohydrates 0.3g; fat 7.4g; cholesterol 13.6mg; sodium 351.7mg.

# CHAPTER 3: GRILL LAMB RECIPES

# -LEG OF LAMB

## Servings:
9
## Yield:
8 -10 servings

8 pounds whole leg of lamb
salt to taste
ground black pepper to taste
6 ounces prepared mustard
1 dash Worcestershire sauce
2 tablespoons all-purpose flour
4 cloves garlic, sliced (Optional)

1
Preheat oven to 325 degrees F (165 degrees C).

2
Generously salt and pepper lamb. Smear the mustard all over
the lamb and sprinkle it with a fine coating of flour. Place
lamb in a roasting pan and place slices of garlic over top.
Sprinkle with Worcestershire sauce to taste.

3
Roast uncovered at 325 degrees F (165 degrees C) until
desired doneness. About 20 minutes per pound for a pink
roast. Remove from pan to a heated platter. Use the drippings
to make a gravy by a little flour and water. Season with salt
and pepper.

## Nutrition:

Per Serving: 476 calories; protein 46.1g; carbohydrates 2.8g; fat 29.8g; cholesterol 164mg; sodium 328.9mg.

# -LOIN LAMB CHOPS

**Prep Time:**
5 mins
**Cook Time:**
10 mins
Additional:
1 hr 5 mins
**Total Time:**
1 hr 20 mins
**Servings:**
4
**Yield:**
4 servings

2 tablespoons herbes de Provence
1 ½ tablespoons olive oil
2 cloves garlic, minced
2 teaspoons lemon juice
8 (5 ounce) lamb loin chops
1 pinch salt and freshly ground black pepper

1

Combine herbes de Provence, olive oil, garlic, and lemon juice in a small bowl. Rub mixture over lamb chops and refrigerate for at least 1 hour.

2

Preheat an outdoor grill for medium-high heat and lightly oil the grate.

3

Season chops with salt and pepper.

4

Place chops on the preheated grill and cook until browned and medium-rare on the inside, 3 to 4 minutes per side. Remove from grill and place on an aluminum foil-covered plate to rest for 5 minutes before serving.

## Nutrition:

Per Serving: 579 calories; protein 42.5g; carbohydrates 0.7g; fat 43.9g; cholesterol 168.3mg; sodium 168.7mg.

# CHAPTER 4: **GRILL POULTRY RECIPES**

# -BBQ SIMPLE TURKEY SANDWICHES

**Prep Time:**
20 mins
**Cook Time:**
8 hrs
**Total Time:**
8 hrs 20 mins
**Servings:**
6
**Yield:**
6 servings

2 turkey legs without skin
½ cup firmly packed brown sugar
¼ cup prepared yellow mustard
1 tablespoon liquid smoke flavoring
2 tablespoons ketchup
2 tablespoons apple cider vinegar
2 tablespoons hot pepper sauce
1 teaspoon salt
1 teaspoon coarse ground black pepper
1 teaspoon crushed red pepper flakes

1

Spray the inside of a slow cooker with nonstick cooking spray, and place the turkey legs into the cooker. In a bowl, mix together the brown sugar, yellow mustard, smoke flavoring, ketchup, cider vinegar, hot pepper sauce, salt, black pepper, and red pepper flakes until the sugar has dissolved. Pour the mixture over the turkey legs.

2

Cover the cooker, set to Low, and cook 8 to 10 hours. Remove the turkey legs from the cooker, separate meat from bones and tendons, and shred the meat; return the meat to the sauce for serving.

**Nutrition:**
Per Serving: 279 calories; protein 32.7g; carbohydrates 20.3g; fat 6.9g; cholesterol 130.5mg; sodium 779.2mg.

# -ROAST SPATCHCOCK TURKEY

**Prep Time:**
15 mins
**Cook Time:**
1 hr 45 mins
Additional:
10 mins
**Total Time:**
2 hrs 10 mins
**Servings:**
10
**Yield:**
1 10-pound turkey

1 (10 pound) whole turkey
½ cup olive oil
1 tablespoon salt
1 tablespoon chopped fresh sage
1 tablespoon fresh thyme leaves
1 tablespoon finely chopped fresh rosemary
1 teaspoon crushed black pepper

1

Preheat oven to 350 degrees F (175 degrees C). Place a roasting rack on a baking sheet.

2

Turn the turkey over, breast-side down. Using a pair of sharp heavy-duty kitchen shears, cut along one side of the backbone. Repeat on the other side of the backbone. Reserve the backbone for making turkey stock for gravy. Press firmly down onto both sides of turkey to flatten.

3

Tuck the wing tips under the turkey and place on the roasting rack. Pat skin dry and rub olive oil over the entire turkey; season with salt, sage, thyme, rosemary, and black pepper.

4

Bake in the preheated oven for 1 hour 30 minutes, rotating baking sheet every 30 minutes. Increase temperature to 400 degrees F (200 degrees C) and roast until skin is crisp, about 15 minutes more. An instant-read thermometer inserted into the thickest part of the thigh should read 165 degrees F (74 degrees C). Remove turkey from the oven, cover loosely with a doubled sheet of aluminum foil, and allow to rest for 10 to 15 minutes before slicing.

**Nutrition:**
Per Serving: 777 calories; protein 92g; carbohydrates 0.3g; fat 42.7g; cholesterol 268.2mg; sodium 920.5mg.

# -Spatchcocked Turkey with Herbed Butter

Preparation time: 45 minutes
Brine time: 8-12 hours
Cook time: 4 hours
Smoker temperature: 240°F
Meat finish temperature: 160°F
Recommended wood: Pecan and/or Hickory

Ingredients
12-14 lb turkey
Turkey brine
Herbed butter
Jeff's Texas rub

1:
Remove the turkey from it's packaging.
Remove giblets, neck, pop-up timer and any plastic or
hardware that is holding the legs together.
Place the turkey on your cutting board with the backbone
facing up and neck end toward you.
Using a pair of heavy duty kitchen shears, cut along both sides
of the backbone to completely remove it from the turkey.
Turn the turkey breast side up and press down with both
hands to flatten it.
2:
Make a simple turkey brine using 1 gallon of cold water, 1 cup
of coarse kosher salt and ¾ cup of dark brown sugar. (the
sugar is optional but I think it adds a lot to the brine).
Pour the salt into the water and stir until it becomes clear
again. Add the sugar and stir until it dissolves. Double or
triple the brine recipe as required.

Place the turkey in a plastic, glass or stainless steel container and pour the brine over the bird to cover.

Place a lid or cover on the container with the bird and the brine and place it in the refrigerator overnight or 8-12 hours.

3:

When the turkey is finished brining, discard the brine and rinse the turkey really well under cold water.

Dry the inside and outside of the turkey with clean paper towels.

Place the turkey in the fridge uncovered for about 2 hours to allow the skin to dry further.

While the drying process is occurring, make up the herb butter (recipe below)

4:

Combine 1 stick of softened butter, 1/4 cup chopped parsley, 1/4 cup chopped thyme, 1/4 cup chopped chives, 1/4 cup onion, 5 garlic cloves, 2 TBS Jeff's Texas Rub

If made ahead, allow it to soften to help with the application.

5:

Split the butter into (2) parts and put half of it under the skin and half of it on the outside of the skin.

Work your hands between the skin and the meat tearing the membrane loose as you go. Do this carefully and patiently and you will be able to completely loosen the skin from the breast meat and even the thighs and legs. Leave the skin attached around the edges (except for where your hand entered) to help hold in the butter and herbs.

Once the skin is loose enough, stuff some of the herbed butter in the breast area, the thighs, and the legs. Pat it down from the outside to spread it out a little more.

Apply the remaining herbed butter on the outside of the skin.

6:

Season the entire turkey skin side and meat side with my Texas rub for perfect seasoning throughout.

7:

Set up your smoker for cooking at about 240°F.

If your smoker has a water pan, it's a great idea to use as this helps to reduce the drying effect of the heat.

Make sure you have enough smoking wood to last for at least 2 hours.

Place the spatchcocked turkey skin side up and let it smoke cook for about 4 hours at 240°F.

Monitor the temperature of the breast at it's thickest part and when it reaches about 158-160 it's time to move it from the heat.

8:

Quickly tent some foil over the bird and leave it for about 10-15 minutes to rest before carving.

To carve, remove the leg quarters then separate the thigh from the leg. Remove the wings then remove the breast meat in one big section by cutting along the carcass as you pull back on the breast meat. Slice the breast meat into pieces and you are ready to eat.

# CHAPTER 5: TURKEY, RABBIT AND VEAL

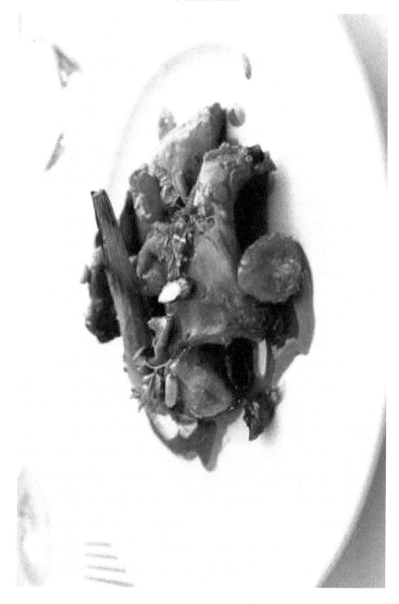

# -SMOKED BEER-CAN TURKEY

## YIELD:
serves 8 to 10
ACTIVE TIME:
1 hour
TOTAL TIME:
16 hours

Ingredients
For the Brine
2 quarts apple Juice
1 cup kosher salt
1/2 cup brown sugar
1/4 cup molasses
3 quarts ice cold water

1 whole natural turkey, 12 to 14 pounds

For the Rub
1 tablespoon paprika
1 teaspoon Kosher salt
1 teaspoon chili powder
1 teaspoon garlic powder
1 teaspoon freshly ground black pepper
1/2 teaspoon onion powder
1/2 teaspoon dried thyme
1/2 teaspoon dried oregano
1/4 teaspoon ground cumin
1/4 teaspoon cayenne pepper

1 medium chunk of apple wood or other light smoking wood
1 (24 ounce) tall can of beer

1.

To make the brine: Whisk together apple juice, salt, brown sugar, and molasses in a large container until salt and sugar are dissolved. Stir in 3 quarts ice cold water. Submerge turkey, breast side down, in brine. Place container in refrigerator and brine for 12 hours.

2.

To make the rub: In a small bowl combine paprika, salt, chili powder, garlic powder, black pepper, onion powder, thyme, oregano, cumin, and cayenne pepper. Set aside.

3.

Remove turkey from brine. Pat dry inside and out with paper towels. Using fingers, gently separate skin from meat underneath breasts and around thighs. Spread about 1 1/2 tablespoon of rub under breast and thigh. Sprinkle remaining rub all over turkey, inside and out.

4.

Fire up smoker or grill to 325°F, adding smoking wood chunks when at temperature. When the wood is ignited and producing smoke, drink or empty 1/3 of beer and place can on smoker. Carefully lower turkey onto beer can, legs down. Adjust turkey legs so it stands vertical stably. Cover and smoke until an instant read thermometer registers 160°F in the thickest part of the breast, about 2 to 3 hours.

5.

Remove the turkey from the smoker and allow to rest, uncovered, for 20 to 30 minutes. Remove beer can; carve and serve.

## -BACON WRAPPED TURKEY

**Prep Time:**
30 mins
**Cook Time:**
3 hrs 30 mins
**Total Time:**
4 hrs
**Servings:**
32
**Yield:**
1 16-pound turkey

¼ cup dried sage
2 tablespoons garlic powder
1 (16 pound) whole turkey, neck and giblets removed
2 (12 ounce) packages bacon
2 cups water

1
Preheat oven to 350 degrees F (175 degrees C).

2
Sprinkle sage and garlic powder over the entire turkey. Wrap turkey completely with bacon. Place turkey on a roasting rack and place roasting rack in a large baking dish. Pour water into the base of the dish.

3
Bake turkey in the preheated oven, basting every 45 minutes with juices in baking dish, until no longer pink at the bone and the juices run clear, 3 1/2 to 4 hours. An instant-read

thermometer inserted into the thickest part of the thigh should read 165 degrees F (74 degrees C).

Per Serving: 381 calories; protein 48.7g; carbohydrates 0.6g; fat 18.9g; cholesterol 141.8mg; sodium 273.5mg.

## -Chicken Wings with Hoisin Sauce and Honey

**Prep Time:**
15 mins
**Cook Time:**
35 mins
Additional:
2 hrs
**Total Time:**
2 hrs 50 mins
**Servings:**
8
**Yield:**
2 pounds

2 cups water
½ cup salt
1 teaspoon garlic powder
1 teaspoon ground ginger
1 teaspoon ground black pepper
2 pounds chicken wings
¼ cup hoisin sauce
3 teaspoons honey
1 tablespoon chopped garlic
1 tablespoon chopped ginger
¼ teaspoon crushed red pepper
2 tablespoons toasted sesame seeds

1

Combine water and salt in a large resealable plastic bag. Add garlic powder, ground ginger, and black pepper. Add chicken wings. Remove excess air and seal bag. Place in the refrigerator for 2 hours. Remove chicken from brine and drain in a colander. Rinse and pat dry.

2

Preheat the oven to 350 degrees F (175 degrees C). Grease a broiling pan.

3

Combine hoisin sauce, honey, garlic, chopped ginger, and crushed red pepper in a large bowl. Add chicken and mix well to coat. Let sit while you toast sesame seeds.

4

Heat a nonstick pan over medium heat and add sesame seeds. Shake and cook until lightly toasted, 1 to 3 minutes. Transfer to a plate lined with a paper towel to cool.

5

Transfer wings to the prepared broiling pan, reserving sauce in the bowl.

6

Bake in the preheated oven for 30 minutes, basting every 10 minutes with reserved sauce. Remove wings from the oven and baste again with sauce.

7

Set an oven rack about 6 inches from the heat source and turn on the oven's broiler. Broil wings until slightly charred, 2 to 3 minutes per side.

8

Serve topped with toasted sesame seeds.

## **Nutrition:**

Per Serving: 126 calories; protein 8.5g; carbohydrates 7.4g; fat 7g; cholesterol 24.1mg; sodium 5992mg.

# CHAPTER 6: SMOKING RECIPES

## -SMOKED BRISKET

**Prep Time:**
10 mins
**Cook Time:**
6 hrs 15 mins
Additional:
8 hrs 30 mins
**Total Time:**
14 hrs 55 mins
**Servings:**
12
**Yield:**
12 servings

5 pounds beef brisket, trimmed of fat
3 tablespoons mustard, or as needed
2 tablespoons brisket rub (such as Fiesta®), or as needed

1

Coat beef brisket with mustard. Cover with brisket rub. Let marinate in the refrigerate, 8 hours to overnight.

2

Remove brisket from the refrigerator and bring to room temperature.

3

Preheat a smoker to 220 degrees F (104 degrees F) according to manufacturer's instructions.

4

Place beef brisket in the smoker and smoke until easily pierced with a knife and an instant-read thermometer inserted into the center reads 190 degrees F (88 degrees C), 6 1/4 to 7 1/2 hours.

5

Wrap brisket with aluminum foil and let rest for 30 minutes before slicing.

**Nutrition:**

Per Serving: 246 calories; protein 22.4g; carbohydrates 0.7g; fat 16.3g; cholesterol 76.9mg; sodium 556.3mg

# -SMOKED BEANS

**Prep Time:**
20 mins
**Cook Time:**
1 hr 10 mins
**Total Time:**
1 hr 30 mins
**Servings:**
12
**Yield:**
12 servings

¾ pound bacon
1 pound ground beef
2 large onions, chopped
1 (18 ounce) bottle honey barbecue sauce
4 (15 ounce) cans pork and beans
1 (15 ounce) can kidney beans, rinsed and drained
1 (15 ounce) can lima beans, rinsed and drained
1 (15 ounce) can black beans, rinsed and drained
½ cup packed brown sugar
3 tablespoons cider vinegar
1 tablespoon liquid smoke flavoring (Optional)
1 teaspoon salt
½ teaspoon ground black pepper

1
Preheat oven to 350 degrees F (175 degrees C).

2
Place the bacon in a large, deep skillet, and cook over
medium-high heat, turning occasionally, until evenly

browned, about 10 minutes. Drain the bacon slices on a paper towel-lined plate. Let cool, and crumble.

3

Place the ground beef and onions into a large skillet over medium heat, and cook and stir until the meat is no longer pink, breaking the meat apart as it cooks, about 10 minutes. Drain excess grease. Transfer the beef and onion mixture into a large Dutch oven. Stir in the crumbled bacon, honey barbecue sauce, pork and beans, kidney beans, lima beans, black beans, brown sugar, cider vinegar, liquid smoke, salt, and pepper.

4

Cover, and bake in the preheated oven until bubbling, about 1 hour.

**Nutrition:**

Per Serving: 449 calories; protein 21.2g; carbohydrates 67.5g; fat 11.7g; cholesterol 43.2mg; sodium 1528.2mg.

# -SMOKED TROUT

**Prep Time:**
5 mins
Additional:
30 mins
**Total Time:**
35 mins
**Servings:**
8
**Yield:**
8 servings

8 ounces smoked trout, skin removed, flaked
8 ounces cream cheese
⅓ cup sour cream
1 green onion, finely chopped
1 tablespoon Worcestershire sauce
1 teaspoon garlic powder
1 teaspoon paprika
½ teaspoon lemon juice
½ teaspoon prepared horseradish (Optional)
1 pinch cayenne pepper
ground black pepper to taste

1

Combine trout, cream cheese, sour cream, green onion,
Worcestershire sauce, garlic powder, paprika, lemon juice,
horseradish, cayenne pepper, and black pepper in a bowl; stir
until blended. Cover and refrigerate for 30 minutes.

## Nutrition:

Per Serving: 177 calories; protein 10.5g; carbohydrates 2.3g; fat 14g; cholesterol 57.8mg; sodium 111.4mg.

# CHAPTER 7: FISH AND SEAFOOD RECIPES

## -Smoked Oysters on the Half "Shell"

**Total Time:**
10 mins
**Yield:**
Serves 10

About 25 large salted potato chips

2 cans (3 oz. each) smoked oysters

5 to 6 tsp. sour cream

2 teaspoons chopped chives

1
Lay chips on a serving plate. Top each with an oyster, cut in half if large, about 1/4 tsp. sour cream, and a sprinkle of chives.

2
Note: Nutritional analysis is per serving.

**Nutrition:**
Per Serving: 115 calories; calories from fat 61%; protein 3.6g; fat 7.8g; saturated fat 2.4g; carbohydrates 9.5g; fiber 1.7g; sodium 151mg; cholesterol 13mg

# -BARBECUED SHRIMP

**Prep Time:**

10 mins

**Cook Time:**

25 mins

**Total Time:**

35 mins

**Servings:**

12

**Yield:**

12 servings

2 cups butter

2 cups olive oil

¾ cup Worcestershire sauce

6 tablespoons ground black pepper

4 lemons, sliced

½ teaspoon hot pepper sauce

1 teaspoon Italian seasoning

3 cloves garlic, minced

1 teaspoon paprika

4 teaspoons salt

8 pounds large shrimp - peeled and deveined

1

Preheat oven to 450 degrees F (230 degrees C).

2

Heat butter and oil in a large saucepan. Add Worcestershire sauce, black pepper, lemons, hot sauce, Italian seasoning, garlic, paprika and salt to the saucepan. Mix well and simmer 5 to 7 minutes.

3

Divide shrimp between two Dutch ovens. Pour 1/2 of the sauce into one Dutch oven and 1/2 of the sauce into the other. Heat the sauce in both Dutch ovens to a simmer and cook the shrimp for 6 to 8 minutes; until the shrimp begin to turn pink.

4

When the shrimp have begun to turn pink pour the shrimp and sauce from both Dutch ovens into a large baking pan (or two pans depending on how much sauce you have). Bake the shrimp for 10 minutes, stirring once.

Per Serving: 854 calories; protein 50.6g; carbohydrates 9.7g; fat 69.5g; cholesterol 542.2mg; sodium 1697.6mg

# -FISH STEW

**Prep Time:**
15 mins
**Cook Time:**
30 mins
**Total Time:**
45 mins
**Servings:**
4
**Yield:**
4 servings

1 (15 ounce) can mackerel, undrained
1 (10.75 ounce) can tomato soup (not condensed) (Optional)
4 potatoes, sliced
1 onion, sliced
red pepper flakes (to taste)
1 egg (Optional)

1
Place undrained mackerel, tomato soup (if using), potatoes, onion, and red pepper flakes in a medium stock pot. Add just enough water to cover.

2
Bring to a boil over medium-high heat, reduce to a simmer, and cook 30 minutes, or until potatoes are tender.

3
Break the egg over the stew, if desired, and serve.

## Nutrition:

Per Serving: 339 calories; protein 27.2g; carbohydrates 40.9g; fat 7.3g; cholesterol 117.9mg; sodium 393.7mg.

# -TUNA BURGER

**Prep Time:**
15 mins
**Cook Time:**
10 mins
**Total Time:**
25 mins
**Servings:**
4
**Yield:**
4 tuna burgers

1 (7 ounce) pouch tuna in water, drained and juice reserved
3 tablespoons finely chopped onion
3 tablespoons finely chopped celery with leaves
1 large egg
¼ cup dry bread crumbs
2 slices day-old bread, cubed
1 pinch garlic powder, or to taste
1 pinch salt and ground black pepper to taste
3 tablespoons olive oil

1

Mix drained tuna, onion, celery, egg, bread crumbs, bread cubes, garlic powder, salt, and black pepper in a bowl. If mixture is too dry to hold together, stir in reserved tuna juice, 1 teaspoon at a time. Divide mixture in fourths and shape each portion into a patty.

2

Heat olive oil in a large skillet over medium heat and pan-fry the patties until golden brown, about 3 minutes per side. Drain patties on paper towels.

## Nutrition:

Per Serving: 230 calories; protein 16.2g; carbohydrates 12.3g; fat 12.6g; cholesterol 61.4mg; sodium 220.7mg.

# CHAPTER 8: VEGETARIAN RECIPES

## -WATERMELON SOUP

**Prep Time:**
15 mins
Additional:
2 hrs
**Total Time:**
2 hrs 15 mins
**Servings:**
3
**Yield:**
3 servings

4 cups cubed seeded watermelon
2 tablespoons lemon juice
1 tablespoon chopped fresh mint
1 tablespoon honey

1

Blend watermelon, lemon juice, mint, and honey in a blender until smooth. Refrigerate 2 hours before serving.

**Nutrition:**
Per Serving: 85 calories; protein 1.3g; carbohydrates 22g; fat 0.3g; sodium 2.4mg.

# -GRILLED CARROTS

**Prep Time:**
10 mins
**Cook Time:**
15 mins
**Total Time:**
25 mins
**Servings:**
4
**Yield:**
4 servings

1 pound carrots, peeled and trimmed
1 tablespoon olive oil
salt and pepper to taste
1 tablespoon maple syrup

1
Preheat an outdoor grill for medium-high heat and lightly oil
the grate.

2
Brush carrots with olive oil and sprinkle with salt and pepper.

3
Place carrots on the grill, perpendicular to the grates. Reduce
heat to medium and cook, turning them regularly, until
carrots have started to caramelize and are cooked throughout,
14 to 18 minutes. Move them to indirect heat and continue
cooking if they start burning.

4

Brush carrots with maple syrup and grill 1 minute more before transferring to a plate. Serve immediately.

## Nutrition:

Per Serving: 89 calories; protein 1.1g; carbohydrates 14.2g; fat 3.7g; sodium 117.6mg.

# -PARMESAN ROASTED CAULIFLOWER

**Prep Time:**
10 mins
**Cook Time:**
10 mins
**Total Time:**
20 mins
**Servings:**
4
**Yield:**
4 servings

1 head cauliflower, cut into small florets
1 teaspoon salt
1 teaspoon mixed herbs
½ teaspoon ground black pepper
3 tablespoons olive oil
½ cup grated Parmesan cheese

1

Preheat oven to 450 degrees F (230 degrees C). Line a baking sheet with aluminum foil.

2

Arrange cauliflower on the prepared baking sheet. Sprinkle with salt, mixed herbs, and pepper. Drizzle with olive oil; toss until well coated. Sprinkle Parmesan cheese on top.

3

Roast in the preheated oven until crisp, 10 to 15 minutes.

## Nutrition:

Per Serving: 171 calories; protein 6.8g; carbohydrates 8.4g; fat 13.2g; cholesterol 8.8mg; sodium 777.9mg.

# CHAPTER 9: RED MEAT RECIPES

## -GRILLED PORTERHOUSE STEAK WITH CHIMICHURRI SAUCE

**Prep Time:**
15 mins
**Cook Time:**
30 mins
Additional:
40 mins
**Total Time:**
1 hr 25 mins
**Servings:**
4
**Yield:**
4 servings

Steak:
4 pounds porterhouse steak
1 tablespoon extra-virgin olive oil, or more as needed
1 pinch kosher salt, or to taste
1 pinch ground black pepper, or to taste
Chimichurri Sauce:
1 shallot, chopped
4 cloves garlic, chopped
1 cup fresh flat-leaf parsley leaves
2 tablespoons fresh oregano leaves
½ teaspoon red pepper flakes
1 pinch kosher salt, or more to taste
1 pinch ground black pepper, or more to taste
¼ cup red wine vinegar
¼ cup extra-virgin olive oil

1 tablespoon water

1

Bring steak to room temperature 30 minutes prior to grilling. Preheat an indoor grill to medium heat and lightly oil the grate.

2

Brush steak with olive oil and season with salt and pepper. Grill until slightly charred, firm, and reddish-pink and juicy in the center, about 11 minutes per side. Hold steak with tongs to sear edges. An instant-read thermometer inserted into the center should read 130 degrees F (54 degrees C). Transfer steak to a cutting board; cover loosely with aluminum foil, and let rest for 10 minutes.

3

Meanwhile, pulse shallot, garlic, parsley, oregano, red pepper flakes, kosher salt and pepper together in a food processor until roughly chopped. Add red wine vinegar, olive oil, and water; pulse to a textured sauce. Transfer to a serving bowl.

4

Slice steak and serve with prepared chimichurri sauce.

## Nutrition:

Per Serving: 745 calories; protein 47.9g; carbohydrates 5.9g; fat 57.6g; cholesterol 136.8mg; sodium 339.8mg.

# -TERIYAKI RIB EYE STEAK

**Prep Time:**
10 mins
**Cook Time:**
15 mins
Additional:
2 hrs
**Total Time:**
2 hrs 25 mins
**Servings:**
2
**Yield:**
2 servings

2 tablespoons soy sauce
2 tablespoons water
1 tablespoon white sugar
1 ½ teaspoons honey
1 ½ teaspoons Worcestershire sauce
1 ¼ teaspoons distilled white vinegar
1 teaspoon olive oil
¼ teaspoon onion powder
¼ teaspoon garlic powder
⅛ teaspoon ground ginger
2 (6 ounce) lean beef rib eye steaks

1

Whisk together the soy sauce, water, sugar, honey,
Worcestershire sauce, vinegar, olive oil, onion powder, garlic
powder, and ground ginger in a large bowl. Pierce steaks
several times with a fork. Marinate steaks in soy sauce
mixture for at least 2 hours.

2

Cook the steaks in a hot skillet, wok, or hibachi over medium heat; 7 minutes per side for medium. An instant-read thermometer inserted into the center should read 140 degrees F (60 degrees C).

## Nutrition:

Per Serving: 297 calories; protein 19.6g; carbohydrates 13.5g; fat 18.1g; cholesterol 60.3mg; sodium 991.6mg.

## -BEER BRAISED LAMB SHANKS

**Prep Time:**
15 mins
**Cook Time:**
3 hrs 10 mins
Additional:
8 hrs 30 mins
**Total Time:**
11 hrs 55 mins
**Servings:**
2
**Yield:**
2 lamb shanks

2 lamb shanks
1 teaspoon salt, divided, or to taste
freshly ground black pepper to taste
1 tablespoon olive oil
1 onion, chopped
2 large carrots, cut into 1-inch pieces
1 large stalk celery, cut into 1-inch pieces
3 cloves garlic, finely chopped
2 teaspoons tomato paste
1 (12 fluid ounce) can or bottle beer
2 sprigs rosemary
1 pinch cayenne pepper

1
Season lamb shanks with salt and pepper.

2

Heat olive oil in a deep-sided pan or pot over medium-high heat. Add lamb and cook, turning as needed, until browned, about 5 minutes. Remove from pan and reduce heat to medium.

3

Place chopped onion, carrot, celery, and garlic in the pan. Season with a large pinch of salt. Cook and stir until vegetable juices start to come out, about 2 minutes. Add tomato paste and stir to coat, about 1 minute. Pour in beer and stir in rosemary. Raise heat to high and bring sauce mixture to a simmer.

4

Toss lamb shanks in with the sauce mixture. Reduce heat to low. Cover and simmer until lamb is nearly fork-tender, flipping lamb after 1 hour, about 2 hours. Remove from heat and let cool to room temperature, at least 30 minutes. Refrigerate, 8 hours to overnight.

5

Skim the fat off the top of the sauce, if desired. Cover and bring lamb to a simmer over low heat. Flip and continue simmering until meat is fork-tender and nearly falling off the bone, about 45 minutes. Place lamb shanks in a bowl to keep warm.

6

Bring sauce to a boil over high heat. Boil until reduced by half but not too thick, about 3 minutes. Season with salt and cayenne pepper. Plate the lamb shanks and spoon sauce on top.

**Nutrition:**

Per Serving: 387 calories; protein 29.8g; carbohydrates 22.4g; fat 14.4g; cholesterol 82.2mg; sodium 1362.8mg.

# CHAPTER 10: **BAKING RECIPES**

# -PRETZELS

**Prep Time:**
40 mins
**Cook Time:**
12 mins
Additional:
1 hr 30 mins
**Total Time:**
2 hrs 22 mins
**Servings:**
12
**Yield:**
12 pretzels

1 (.25 ounce) package active dry yeast
1 cup warm water (100 degrees F/40 degrees C)
1 ½ cups all-purpose flour
2 tablespoons vegetable oil
½ teaspoon table salt
1 ¼ cups all-purpose flour
2 tablespoons baking soda
2 tablespoons coarse salt

1

Sprinkle the yeast over 1 cup of warm water in a bowl. The water should be no more than 100 degrees F (40 degrees C). Let stand for 10 minutes until the yeast softens and begins to form a creamy foam.

2

Stir in 1 1/2 cups of flour, vegetable oil, and table salt, to make a thick, smooth batter. Stir in 1 1/4 cups of flour, and knead the dough on a well-floured surface until elastic, about 5 minutes. Form the dough into a ball, cover it with a cloth, and let it rest for 1 hour.

3

Line a baking sheet with parchment paper.

4

Cut the dough ball into 12 even pieces, and roll each out into a rope about 18 inches long and as thick as a pencil. To shape into pretzels, form a dough piece into a "U" shape, then cross the two tails to make a loop. Spread the two tail ends apart, bring them up, and press the ends into the top of the loop, to form the pretzel shape. Let the formed pretzels rest for 30 minutes on the prepared baking sheet.

5

Preheat an oven to 475 degrees F (245 degrees C).

6

Fill a large saucepan about half full of water, bring to a boil, and stir in the baking soda. Working one at a time, drop each pretzel into the boiling water, and let cook for 1 minute, to give the pretzel a skin. Place the boiled pretzels onto the prepared baking sheet, and sprinkle each one with coarse salt.

7

Bake in the preheated oven until the pretzels are golden brown, about 12 minutes.

**Nutrition:**

Per Serving: 126 calories; protein 3.2g; carbohydrates 22.1g; fat 2.6g; sodium 1645.7mg.

# -Grilled Strawberry Shortcake with Sweet Cream

**Prep Time:**
15 mins
**Cook Time:**
1 hr
Additional:
4 hrs
**Total Time:**
5 hrs 15 mins
**Servings:**
8
**Yield:**
8 servings

Pound Cake:
2 cups all-purpose flour
1 ½ teaspoons baking powder
½ teaspoon salt
¾ cup unsalted butter, room temperature
1 (8 ounce) package cream cheese, softened
1 ½ cups granulated sugar
4 large eggs
2 teaspoons pure vanilla extract
Reynolds Wrap® Non Stick Aluminum Foil

Strawberries:
1 ½ pounds fresh strawberries, hulled and sliced
⅓ cup granulated sugar
8 Reynolds® Aluminum Foil Baking Cups - jumbo

Cream:
1 ½ cups heavy cream

½ cup powdered sugar
1 pinch salt
1 teaspoon pure vanilla extract

1

Preheat oven to 325 degrees F and place a rack in the center of the oven. Line a 9x5-inch baking pan with Reynolds Wrap® Non Stick Aluminum Foil and set aside.

2

Whisk together flour, baking powder and salt in a medium bowl. Set aside.

3

Cream together softened butter and cream cheese in the bowl of an electric stand mixer fitted with a paddle attachment. Stop the mixer occasionally to scrape down the bowl and make sure that the butter and cream cheese are evenly mixed. Add the sugar to the butter and cream cheese mixture, and beat on medium speed until smooth and creamy, about 3 minutes.

4

Beat in one egg at a time, mixing for one minute after each addition. Stop the mixer and scrape down the sides of the bowl as necessary. Beat in vanilla extract.

5

Add dry ingredients all at once. Beat on low speed until dry ingredients are completely incorporated. Spoon batter into prepared pan. Bake for 50 to 60 minutes, rotating once or twice during baking. Bake until a skewer inserted in the center comes out clean or with just a few crumbs. Allow cake to cool in the pan for 15 minutes before inverting onto a wire rack to cool to room temperature. Wrap the cooled cake and refrigerate for 4 hours or overnight.

6

Slice the chilled pound cake into 8 thick slices.

7

Toss the strawberries together with the sugar in a small bowl. Allow to rest at room temperature for 20 minutes.

8

Whip the heavy cream with powdered sugar, salt and vanilla until soft peaks form. Set aside.

9

Grill the slices of pound cake over a warm, greased grill until golden brown grill marks appear on both sides of cake, flipping once.

10

Warm the strawberries on the grill by spooning strawberries among 8 Jumbo Reynolds® Aluminum Foil Baking Cups and warming alongside the pound cake.

11

Serve warm pound cake slices with warmed strawberries and sweet cream.

## Nutrition:
Per Serving: 794 calories; protein 10.2g; carbohydrates 86.7g; fat 46.6g; cholesterol 230.7mg; sodium 395mg.

# -FRENCH EGG AND BACON SANDWICH

**Prep Time:**
5 mins
**Cook Time:**
15 mins
**Total Time:**
20 mins
**Servings:**
2
**Yield:**
2 servings

2 eggs, beaten
4 slices bread
4 slices bacon
2 eggs
½ cup maple syrup

1

Dip bread slices in beaten eggs. Heat a lightly oiled griddle or frying pan over medium high heat. Cook until browned on both sides. Set aside but keep warm.

2

Place bacon in a large, deep skillet. Cook over medium high heat until evenly brown. Drain and set aside. Reserve 1 tablespoon of bacon grease in pan and fry remaining two eggs.

3

Place one piece of French toast on each of two plates. Place the fried eggs on top of the bread, top the eggs with strips of bacon. Cover with the remaining pieces of French toast. Following that by pouring on the syrup.

## Nutrition:

Per Serving: 738 calories; protein 22.9g; carbohydrates 79.3g; fat 37g; cholesterol 410.1mg; sodium 954.1mg.

# CHAPTER 11: **CHEESE AND BREAD**

# -CHEDDAR CHEESE SAUCE

**Prep Time:**
5 mins
**Cook Time:**
5 mins
**Total Time:**
10 mins
**Servings:**
16
**Yield:**
2 cups

2 tablespoons unsalted butter
2 tablespoons all-purpose flour
¼ teaspoon salt
1 cup whole milk
1 ¾ cups shredded sharp Cheddar cheese

1

Melt butter in a saucepan over medium heat. Whisk in flour and salt until a paste forms. Slowly add milk; cook and stir until fully incorporated, about 2 minutes. Add cheese, stir to combine, and cook until melted, 1 to 2 minutes.

**Nutrition:**
Per Serving: 75 calories; protein 3.7g; carbohydrates 1.6g; fat 6g; cholesterol 18.3mg; sodium 119.4mg

## -SCANDIVIAN ALMOND BREAD

**Prep Time:**
20 mins
**Cook Time:**
50 mins
Additional:
1 hr 15 mins
**Total Time:**
2 hrs 25 mins
**Servings:**
12
**Yield:**
12 servings

½ cup butter
1 ¼ cups white sugar
1 egg
½ teaspoon baking powder
1 ½ teaspoons almond extract
⅔ cup heavy cream
1 ¼ cups all-purpose flour

1

Preheat an oven to 350 degrees F (175 degrees C). Line a loaf pan with wax paper, then spray with cooking spray.

2

Place the butter into a heavy saucepan, and melt over medium heat. Allow the butter to simmer until foam rises to the top of the butter, 5 to 10 minutes. Gently skim away the foam and discard; pour the golden, clear layer of butter through a fine mesh strainer into a bowl to remove remaining milk solids, avoiding pouring any milk solids left in the bottom of the pan. Allow the clarified butter to cool.

### 3

Beat sugar and egg with an electric mixer in a large bowl until light and fluffy. Beat in the baking powder and almond extract. Stir in the clarified butter. Pour in the flour alternately with the cream in 2 or 3 installments, mixing until just incorporated. Pour batter into prepared pan.

### 4

Bake in the preheated oven until a toothpick inserted into the center comes out clean, 50 to 60 minutes. Cool in the pan for 15 minutes before removing to cool completely on a wire rack.

**Nutrition:**

Per Serving: 249 calories; protein 2.2g; carbohydrates 31.2g; fat 13.1g; cholesterol 53.9mg; sodium 85.9mg.

# -ROASTED BUTTERNUT SQUASH

**Prep Time:**
15 mins
**Cook Time:**
25 mins
**Total Time:**
40 mins
**Servings:**
4
**Yield:**
4 servings

1 butternut squash - peeled, seeded, and cut into 1-inch cubes
2 tablespoons olive oil
2 cloves garlic, minced
salt and ground black pepper to taste

1
Preheat oven to 400 degrees F (200 degrees C).

2
Toss butternut squash with olive oil and garlic in a large bowl.
Season with salt and black pepper. Arrange coated squash on
a baking sheet.

3
Roast in the preheated oven until squash is tender and lightly
browned, 25 to 30 minutes.

**Nutrition:**

Per Serving: 177 calories; protein 2.6g; carbohydrates 30.3g; fat 7g; sodium 10.6mg.

# CHAPTER 12: **TRADITIONAL RECIPES**

# -GRILLED SALMON

**Prep Time:**
15 mins
**Cook Time:**
15 mins
Additional:
30 mins
**Total Time:**
1 hr
**Servings:**
6
**Yield:**
6 servings

½ cup olive oil
¼ cup lemon juice
4 green onions, thinly sliced
1 tablespoon chopped fresh parsley
1 teaspoon chopped fresh rosemary
1 teaspoon chopped fresh thyme
½ teaspoon salt
⅛ teaspoon black pepper
⅛ teaspoon garlic powder
3 pounds salmon fillets

1

Combine olive oil, lemon juice, green onions, parsley, rosemary, thyme, salt, black pepper, and garlic powder in a small bowl. Set aside 1/4 cup of the marinade. Place salmon in a shallow dish and pour the remaining marinade over the top. Cover and refrigerate for 30 minutes. Remove the salmon and discard the used marinade.

2

Preheat grill for medium heat and lightly oil the grate.

3

Place salmon on the preheated grill skin side down. Cook, basting occasionally with the reserved marinade, until the fish flakes easily with a fork, 15 to 20 minutes.

## Nutrition:

Per Serving: 412 calories; protein 41.8g; carbohydrates 1.8g; fat 25.7g; cholesterol 97.4mg; sodium 299mg.

# -HALIBUT WITH VEGETABLES

**Prep Time:**
15 mins
**Cook Time:**
20 mins
Additional:
10 mins
**Total Time:**
45 mins
**Servings:**
6
**Yield:**
6 servings

2 pounds halibut fillets
salt and pepper to taste
¼ cup olive oil
½ cup chopped fresh parsley
1 yellow onion, thinly sliced
2 stalks celery, chopped
1 green bell pepper, chopped
1 (16 ounce) can diced tomatoes
2 tablespoons capers
4 cloves garlic, minced

1
Preheat oven to 425 degrees F (220 degrees C).

2
Wash halibut and pat dry. Cut into serving size pieces, and
place in a 9x13 inch baking pan. Sprinkle with salt and

pepper. Stir together the olive oil, parsley, onion, celery, bell pepper, tomatoes, capers, and garlic; pour over the halibut.

3

Bake until halibut is slightly opaque in the center, about 20 minutes. Remove from oven; let stand for 10 minutes before serving.

**Nutrition:**

Per Serving: 291 calories; protein 34g; carbohydrates 8.5g; fat 12g; cholesterol 56.3mg; sodium 304.4mg.

## -LEEK AND SALMON SOUP

**Prep Time:**
40 mins
**Cook Time:**
35 mins
**Total Time:**
1 hr 15 mins
**Servings:**
6
**Yield:**
6 servings

2 tablespoons vegetable oil
3 leeks, white and light green parts only, thinly sliced
2 small yellow onions, thinly sliced
2 shallots, thinly sliced
4 cloves garlic, minced
1 teaspoon salt
5 cups vegetable stock, divided
2 large yellow potatoes, sliced
1 small head cauliflower, broken into small florets
2 carrots, sliced
1 cup heavy cream
1 pound skinless salmon fillet, cut into large chunks
salt and cracked black pepper to taste
½ (2.8 ounce) package French-fried onions, or to taste

1
Heat oil in a large pot over medium heat. Add leeks, onions, and shallots. Add garlic and salt. Cook and stir until all is well wilted and soft, but not browned, about 3 minutes.

2

Pour 4 cups of stock into the pot; add potatoes, cauliflower, and carrots. Bring to a boil, reduce heat to low, and cook until carrots and potatoes are soft, about 20 minutes. Insert a hand blender into the soup and blend until creamy-smooth. Add more broth if too thick; the soup should be the consistency of thick bisque.

3

Stir cream into the soup; cook until heated through but not boiling. Add salmon; cook and stir until it flakes apart, 5 to 6 minutes. Season with salt and pepper. Pour into bowls and sprinkle onions on top.

**Nutrition:**

Per Serving: 426 calories; protein 18.7g; carbohydrates 31.1g; fat 25.8g; cholesterol 86.8mg; sodium 782.1mg.

# CHAPTER 13: **SAUCES AND RUBS**

## -BBQ RUB

**Prep Time:**
5 mins
**Total Time:**
5 mins
**Servings:**
24
**Yield:**
Cup

¼ cup paprika
2 tablespoons chili powder
1 teaspoon dry mustard
1 teaspoon meat tenderizer
½ teaspoon onion salt
½ teaspoon garlic salt
½ teaspoon dried basil

1

Mix paprika, chili powder, mustard, meat tenderizer, onion salt, garlic salt, and basil in a bowl.

**Nutrition:**
Per Serving: 7 calories; protein 0.4g; carbohydrates 1.1g; fat 0.3g; sodium 103.1mg.

# -MAYONNAISE

**Prep Time:**
5 mins
**Total Time:**
5 mins
**Servings:**
16
**Yield:**
1 cup

1 egg
½ teaspoon minced garlic
1 tablespoon lemon juice
1 teaspoon prepared yellow mustard
¾ cup vegetable or olive oil
salt and pepper to taste

1

Combine the egg, garlic, lemon juice and mustard in the container of a blender or food processor. Blend until smooth, then blend on low speed while pouring oil into the blender in a fine stream as the mixture emulsifies and thickens.

**Nutrition:**
Per Serving: 95 calories; protein 0.4g; carbohydrates 0.2g; fat 10.5g; cholesterol 11.6mg; sodium 17.7mg

# -BASIL PESTO

**Prep Time:**
15 mins
**Total Time:**
15 mins
**Servings:**
16
**Yield:**
2 cups

4 cups packed fresh basil leaves
1 cup freshly grated Parmigiano-Reggiano cheese
1 cup olive oil
6 cloves garlic, minced
⅔ cup pine nuts (Optional)
salt and ground black pepper to taste

1

Combine basil, Parmigiano-Reggiano cheese, and olive oil in a food processor. Pulse to combine. Add garlic, pine nuts, salt, and pepper. Pulse until mixture becomes smooth and blended.

2

Pour mixture onto a large sheet of plastic wrap; roll into a tube shape and seal. Store in the refrigerator until needed.

**Nutrition:**
Per Serving: 177 calories; protein 3.7g; carbohydrates 1.7g; fat 17.9g; cholesterol 4.4mg; sodium 87.2mg.

CPSIA information can be obtained
at www.ICGtesting.com
Printed in the USA
BVHW091657120521
607126BV00006B/810